Oxford
UNIVERSITY PRESS

Oxford International Primary History

Specimen Copy
Not for Sale

3

Pat Lunt

Oxford International Primary for enquiring minds

OXFORD

OXFORD
UNIVERSITY PRESS

Great Clarendon Street, Oxford, OX2 6DP, United Kingdom

Oxford University Press is a department of the University of Oxford. It furthers the University's objective of excellence in research, scholarship, and education by publishing worldwide. Oxford is a registered trade mark of Oxford University Press in the UK and in certain other countries.

© Pat Lunt 2017

The moral rights of the author have been asserted.

First published in 2017

All rights reserved. No part of this publication may be reproduced, stored in a retrieval system, or transmitted, in any form or by any means, without the prior permission in writing of Oxford University Press, or as expressly permitted by law, by licence or under terms agreed with the appropriate reprographics rights organization. Enquiries concerning reproduction outside the scope of the above should be sent to the Rights Department, Oxford University Press, at the address above.

You must not circulate this work in any other form and you must impose this same condition on any acquirer.

British Library Cataloguing in Publication Data
Data available

ISBN 978-0-19-841811-5

1 3 5 7 9 10 8 6 4 2

Paper used in the production of this book is a natural, recyclable product made from wood grown in sustainable forests. The manufacturing process conforms to the environmental regulations of the country of origin.

Printed in India by Replika Press Pvt.Ltd

Acknowledgements

Cover: Carlo Molinari

Artwork: Aptara

Photos: p4 & p5: Ruth Hofshi/Alamy; **p4 (L) & p19 (L)**: Jaroslav Moravcik/Shutterstock; **p4 (M) & p19 (M)**: John A Davis/Shutterstock; **p4 (R) & p19 (R)**: David Peter Robinson/Shutterstock; **p6**: joppo/Shutterstock; **p10 (T)**: elnavegante/Shutterstock; **p10 (B)**: Granger Historical Picture Archive/Alamy; **p11**: Museo Episcopal de Vic, Osona, Catalonia, Spain/Photo © AISA/Bridgeman Images; **p13**: PRISMA ARCHIVO/Alamy; **p14**: BBA Photography/Shutterstock; **p15**: aslysun/Shutterstock; **p18 & p19**: David Noton Photography/Alamy; **p18 (T)**: Peter Horree/Alamy; **P18 (B)**: Marc Tielemans/Alamy; **p21 (T)**: Jada Images/Alamy; **p21 (B) & p31 (TR)**: Ancient Art and Architecture/Alamy; **p22**: www.BibleLandPictures.com/Alamy; **p23**: Lanmas/Alamy; **p25**: age fotostock/Alamy; **p28 & p31 (B)**: Steve Speller/Alamy; **p31 (TL)**: Lanmas/Alamy; **p32 (L) & p45 (T)**: Fedor Selivanov/Alamy; **p32 (R)**: Peter Horree/Alamy; **p33 (T) & p45 (B)**: Peter Horree/Alamy; **p33 (BR)**: Lihui/Dreamstime; **p33 (BM)**: msaadrasheed/123RF; **p33 (BL), p44, p49 (L) & p50**: PRISMA ARCHIVO/Alamy; **p48 (L)**: Alexey Boldin/Shutterstock; **p48 (M)**: Greg Vaughn/Alamy; **p48 (R)**: Hurst Photo; **p49 (R) & p59**: Soundsnaps/Shutterstock; **p51**: B Christopher/Alamy; **p52 (T)**: Allister Mackrell/Alamy; **p52 (B)**: View Stock/Alamy; **p54**: Niday Picture Library/Alamy; **p55 (T)**: Ian Robinson/Alamy; **p55 (B)**: Christopher Godfrey/Alamy; **p57 (L) & p61 (L)**: B Christopher/Alamy; **p57 (ML) & p61 (TM)**: Adrien Veczan/Alamy; **p57 (M) & p61 (TR)**: UrbanImages/Alamy; **p57 (MR) & p61 (ML)**: Billion Photos/Shutterstock; **p57 (R) & p61 (MR)**: Y H Lim/Alamy; **p57 (B)**: Granger Historical Picture Archive/Alamy; **p58 (T)**: MARKA/Alamy; **p58 (B) & p61 (B)**: Everett Collection/Shutterstock; **p59** from top to bottom: INTERFOTO/Alamy; INTERFOTO/Alamy; INTERFOTO/Alamy; NTERFOTO/Alamy; Scanrail1/Shutterstock; **p60**: PRISMA ARCHIVO/Alamy

Although we have made every effort to trace and contact all copyright holders before publication this has not been possible in all cases. If notified, the publisher will rectify any errors or omissions at the earliest opportunity.

Links to third party websites are provided by Oxford in good faith and for information only. Oxford disclaims any responsibility for the materials contained in any third party website referenced in this work.

Contents

1 From hunter-gatherers to village people

1.1	Life in the Stone Age	6
1.2	Food and shelter in the Stone Age	8
1.3	Stone Age art and craft	10
1.4	Farming changes the world	12
1.5	Living in one place	14
1 Review		16

2 The Metal Ages

2.1	Technology in the Bronze Age	20
2.2	Towns, trade and travel	22
2.3	Life and death in the Iron Age	24
2.4	Iron Age settlements	26
2.5	Fighting tribes or traders?	28
2 Review		30

3 Early civilisations

3.1	Early civilisations	34
3.2	Farming and food	36
3.3	City life in the early civilisations	38
3.4	Writing and number systems	40
3.5	Trade and war	42
3 Review		44

4 A history of communication

4.1	Writing and writing tools	48
4.2	Printing	50
4.3	Staying in touch	52
4.4	Telecommunication	54
4.5	Mass communication	56
4 Review		58

Vocabulary quiz 60
Glossary 62

1 From hunter-gatherers to village people

In this unit you will:
- discuss how people lived long ago
- explore how people first began farming
- discuss similarities and differences between life in the past and life now
- explain how we use evidence to find out about Stone Age people

The Stone Age c12 000 BCE–2500 BCE

The Bronze Age c3800 BCE–1200 BCE

The Iron Age c1200 BCE–43 CE

12 000 BCE

43 CE

People have lived on Earth for a very long time. The way in which people lived long ago was very different from how we live today. Paintings on the walls of caves show us some things about life thousands of years ago. What do you think it was like to live thousands of years ago?

Stone Age   prehistoric
hunter-gatherers
settlement   pottery

? **Stone Age** people had not yet invented writing. Stone Age people sometimes painted pictures on cave walls. Which animals can you see in this cave painting?

1 From hunter-gatherers to village people

5

1.1 Life in the Stone Age

Long ago, life was very different. There were no houses to live in. They were no shops selling food or clothes. How did people survive?

What was the Stone Age?

For thousands of years people had to make everything they needed. They used materials they could find. The material people used most to make tools was stone. The Stone Age ended when people learned to make tools from metal. The Stone Age is a **prehistoric** period of time. Prehistoric means the time before people learned to write, so there are no written records of this time.

Stone Age people used different types of stone to make tools. They hit stones against each other to break off smaller pieces with sharp edges. They used the sharp pieces as axes and knives. Over time, people became more skilled and learned to make smaller stone objects such as arrow heads.

What does this ancient picture tell us about life in the Stone Age?

Stone arrow heads

A timeline of the Stone Age

About 11 500 BCE Last Ice Age ends

Palaeolithic
The Early Stone Age

Mesolithic
The Middle Stone Age

About 8000 BCE Farming develops in the Near East

About 4000 BCE Farming first develops in Britain

People also used other materials such as animal skins and bones. They used the skins to make clothing and shelters. They used large animal bones as hammers.

What did people eat in the Stone Age?

People in the Stone Age worked hard just to survive. The most important task was to find enough food. People hunted animals for meat. People who lived near water caught fish.

Stone Age people also gathered food from different plants. They ate fruit, nuts, berries, green plants, roots and wild grain.

We call these people **hunter-gatherers**.

Living together

Hunting large animals was too difficult for one person to do alone. A group of people working together could also gather more food from plants. For these reasons we think that Stone Age people lived together in groups.

Did you know?

A person who studies past human life, by looking at objects and other evidence, is called an archeologist.

Glossary words

archeologist   material
axe   timeline

Activities

1 Work with a partner. Talk about the tools that people use today to make things and to cook. Then write a list of the tools you think Stone Age people made.

2 In a group, compare the food that people ate in the Stone Age with the food we eat today. Discuss how it is the same and how it is different.

Challenge

Use the information in this book and further research to find out about, draw and label three Stone Age tools.

3300 BCE Bronze Age begins in India

Neolithic
The Late Stone Age

The Bronze Age

3100 BCE Bronze Age begins in Egypt

1 From hunter-gatherers to village people

7

1.2 Food and shelter in the Stone Age

People in the Stone Age had to hunt for their food. Which animals did they hunt? How did they use the animals? Where did people find shelter to keep warm, dry and safe?

Where did people find food?

Early Stone Age people were nomads. They had to follow the animals they wanted to hunt. They had to find places where they could gather enough food to survive.

Glossary words

Ice Age   nomads   shelter

What did people eat?

The animals that Stone Age people hunted were different depending on where and when the people lived. The Earth's climate did not always stay the same. When the Earth was warmer there were larger areas of forest. When the Earth was colder there were larger areas covered in ice.

During an Ice Age there were large animals such as the woolly mammoth, the woolly rhinoceros, the cave bear and the sabre-toothed tiger. When the last Ice Age ended, the Earth's temperature increased. More forests grew and there were smaller animals such as wolves, bears, deer and wild cattle.

The woolly mammoth had thick fur to keep it warm.

Different places and temperatures also provided different types of plants for food. People, animals and plants could not easily survive in places covered with ice. People and animals moved to live in the warmer places.

How did Stone Age people keep warm?

Hunter-gatherers moved from one place to another. They needed somewhere warm and dry to sleep. In colder areas they sometimes used caves. In warmer places people made shelters. They made a frame of wood or bone and stretched animal skins over it, like a tent.

Fire was very important. People used fire to keep warm and to cook meat. Fire also helped to keep wild animals away. People made small wood fires near the entrance to a cave. They made fires outside temporary shelters and sometimes even inside the shelters.

A cave shelter in the Early Stone Age may have looked like this.

Did you know?

Stone Age people trained wild dogs to help them hunt animals.

Activities

1 Work with a partner.

   a Write a list of all the things you will need to make a simple Stone Age shelter and a fire.

   b Read your list to the class.

   c As a class, discuss how you will get these things.

2 Write two sentences explaining why life was hard for people living in the Stone Age.

Challenge

Use the information in this book and further research to find out about animals that lived in the Stone Age. Choose three of the animals and write two facts about each one.

1.3 Stone Age art and craft

Stone Age people created works of art and decorative objects using paints, bone and clay. What did these paintings, carvings and objects show? Why did Stone Age people wear jewellery? What was their jewellery made from?

What is cave art?

We know a lot about life in the Early Stone Age because people from this time made paintings, drawings and carvings. There are examples of Early Stone Age art in caves and on rocks in different places all around the world.

The pictures often show animals and humans. In some pictures we can see weapons that the humans are carrying.

Sometimes the paintings are just coloured patterns. In some pictures there are people gathered in groups. They may be meeting to plan a hunt. They may be celebrating. No-one knows.

Cave paintings were made to tell stories or to record special events.

Glossary words

charcoal   event

Paints and brushes

Stone Age people had to make their own paints. They used different coloured earth and perhaps charcoal from a fire.

Stone Age people used their hands and fingers to paint. They may have used brushes made from parts of plants.

Art objects

Other art objects from the Stone Age have also been discovered.

These clay bison, found in a cave in France, tell us that Stone Age people created art.

There are drawings of animals scratched onto discs made from bone. There are figures carved from stone and made from clay. Some early clay art objects are over 14 500 years old.

Jewellery

Items of jewellery from the Stone Age include necklaces, bracelets and pins that people may have attached to their clothes. Jewellery was often made from small bones, animal teeth or shells carved into special shapes. These were threaded onto a piece of cord. The cord was made by twisting animal gut, hair or plant fibres together.

Archeologists believe that wearing jewellery showed that a person was important.

Did you know?

A cave painting from 8000 years ago shows a person collecting honey from a bees' nest.

Stone Age jewellery

Activities

1 In a group, discuss what these images from cave paintings might tell us about life in the Stone Age:

   a groups of running animals followed by humans holding weapons

   b a group of people gathered together in a circle.

2 Imagine you have found a piece of Stone Age jewellery. Draw the jewellery and write a description of it. Write about the person you think wore the jewellery long ago.

Challenge

Imagine what a Stone Age person did in an ordinary day. Write a description of the person's day. Then draw a picture like a Stone Age cave painting to show some of the things the person did.

1.4 Farming changes the world

The Neolithic period saw one of the biggest changes in human history. Instead of hunting and gathering all their food, people began to farm. How did farming change the way in which people lived? What foods did they eat and what tasks did they do?

Where and when were the first farmers?

People first started farming about 11 000 years ago. These people lived in Mesopotamia, an area that covered parts of modern-day Iraq and Syria. People planted grain crops and started to domesticate some of the animals they used to hunt. They still gathered food, hunted animals and fished. The change to farming happened slowly. Farming did not reach Europe until about 6000 BCE.

There were many tasks in a Neolithic farming community.

Changing the land

Farmers changed the land around them. They cleared plants and forests to grow their crops. Their animals ate the wild plants. Farmers sometimes dug channels to bring water to their crops. Farmers sometimes built a dam across a river. They sometimes terraced a hillside.

Glossary words

dam	technology
domesticate	terraced
plough	textiles

Changing diet

People who lived on farms ate cereals such as wheat and barley. They grew the cereals instead of only gathering grains from wild plants. Animals such as sheep, goats and cows provided meat and milk.

Be a good historian

Good historians identify 'turning points' in history when things changed completely. Can you say why farming is a turning point?

New technology

Farming led to inventions such as the plough. Other tools improved too. People now polished their stone tools. The polished stone had a smooth surface and a better cutting edge.

People made pots, vases and other items of **pottery**. They used these pots to store and move food and drink.

Early farming communities also developed textiles. The textiles were made from plants such as cotton and flax. Flax was used to make linen. Sheep and goats provided wool.

New jobs

Some people became very good at pottery. This became the special work that they did.

A community sometimes grew more food than it needed. The community used the extra food to trade with other groups. Trading became another new type of work.

Why was using domesticated animals a good way to pull a plough?

This pot was made in about 3200 BCE.

Activities

1 Work in a group. Imagine you are a group of Neolithic people planning to farm a new area.

   a Discuss how you will need to change the local land.

   b Write a list of tasks that people need to do on the farm.

2 Each person in the group chooses a task from activity 1b. Take turns to mime a task for the class to identify.

Challenge

Use books or the Internet to find out when farming started in your country or region. Write about what the farms produced. Write about any other ways in which people got food.

1.5 Living in one place

Farming allowed people to grow most of the food they needed. They did not always have to move around to find food. They began to live in one place. How did this change the way in which they built houses? How did people find all the things they needed?

Settling down

When people began to live in one place they built **settlements**. They chose the site for a new settlement carefully. The site had to be:

- near a supply of water, such as a river, for washing and cooking
- on good soil to grow crops
- on high ground so that it was easy to defend
- near natural resources, such as wood.

Houses and homes

People in permanent settlements needed to build stronger homes. The houses had to last for a long time. Neolithic builders used building materials such as wood, mud and stone. They used thatch or turf to make the roof of a house.

Skara Brae

Skara Brae is a settlement of stone houses on an island off the coast of Scotland. People lived in these houses between 4500 and 5500 years ago. The people farmed the land nearby. They grew crops and kept animals. They collected berries and nuts. They ate fish and shellfish. They dried seaweed and animal dung to use as fuel.

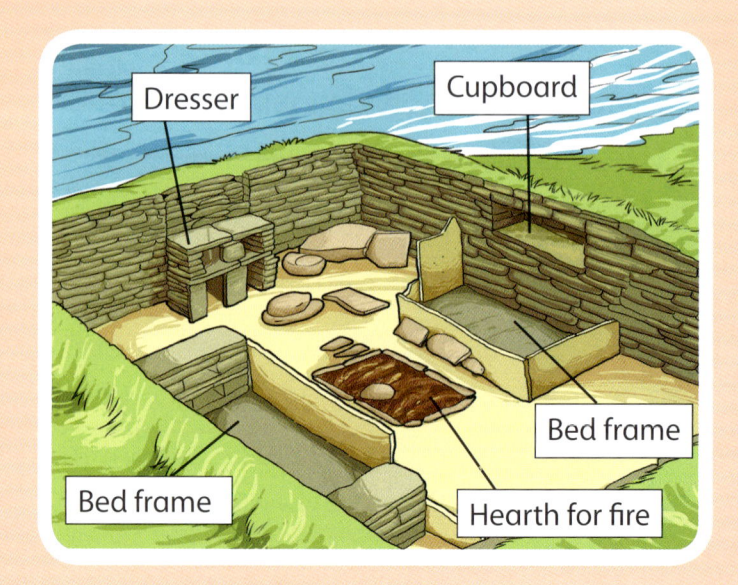

Glossary words

driftwood   scientist   turf
resource   thatch

Neolithic people made the walls of their houses by weaving thin branches between upright posts. They covered the woven branches with plaster made from mud, straw and animal dung.

Dresser — Cupboard — Bed frame — Bed frame — Hearth for fire

Driftwood provided a useful material for tools. Sometimes a whale was stranded on the beach. The whale provided meat, large bones, skin for clothing and teeth for tools and jewellery.

Monuments and burial mounds

Neolithic people built stone monuments. The monuments were often made of huge standing stones arranged in a circle. People were sometimes buried in special mounds called barrows.

Did you know?

Scientists have grown a plant using a seed that was over 30 000 years old.

We do not know for certain what people used monuments like this for. Building them was difficult and took a very long time, so the monuments must have been very important.

Activities

1 With a partner, discuss what these pieces of evidence from Skara Brae tell us:

   a bones of sheep, cattle, red deer and wild boar

   b grains of barley

   c bone tools: shovels, pins and knives

   d small bowls carved from whalebone

   e fish bones and teeth

   f seashells.

2 In a group, discuss different tasks that people had to do in Skara Brae.

3 As a class, write questions to ask a person who lived in Skara Brae. Take turns to be the person from Skara Brae. The other students interview that person.

Challenge

Use books and the Internet to find out about Neolithic settlements in your country or region.

1 From hunter-gatherers to village people

15

1 Review

Answer these questions in your notebook.

Choose the best answer from the choices below. Write a, b or c as your answer.

1. The Stone Age is divided into three periods: the Palaeolithic, the Mesolithic and the:
   a Anaglyptic
   b Neolithic
   c Prehistoric

2. We can find out about prehistoric people by:
   a reading letters they left behind
   b asking older relatives
   c studying objects, paintings and remains from the time

3. A prehistoric arrow head tells us how people of the time:
   a cooked and cleaned
   b hunted and fought
   c relaxed and played

4. In the Early Stone Age people made tools by banging one stone against another to make a sharp edge. People used these tools:
   a as axes and knives
   b as hammers
   c to make jewellery

5. People who move from place to place in search of food and water are called:
   a wanderers
   b settlers
   c nomads

6. When people began to farm they started to:
   a catch fish in nets
   b grow crops for food
   c find wild plants to eat

Decide if these statements are true or false. Write 'True' or 'False' as your answer for each one.

7. The woolly rhinoceros was an animal that lived in the Ice Age.
8. People in the Stone Age made tools and weapons from metal.
9. People learned to farm at the same time all over the world.
10. Early farmers domesticated wild animals to live and work on their farms.

11 After people started farming, they had to move from one place to another.
12 People lived in Skara Brae between 4500 and 5500 years ago.

Now complete these tasks.

13 Write down three things you might see in an Early Stone Age cave shelter. Explain how people might have used these things and what they tell us about life in those times.
14 Write down three ways in which your life is different from the lives of people in the Stone Age and three ways in which it is the same.
15 The picture below shows an imaginary Neolithic farming settlement. Write a list of all the evidence that helps us to know what Neolithic settlements looked like.

1 From hunter-gatherers to village people

2 The Metal Ages

In this unit you will:
- talk about how people lived in the Bronze Age and the Iron Age
- describe how people first began making things from metal
- discuss similarities and differences between life in the past and life in the present day
- explain how we use evidence to find out about people from prehistoric times

? One of these two objects was made almost 4500 years ago. The other was made about 50 years ago. Can you decide which is which? What do you think each object was used for?

An Iron Age hill fort in Dorset, England

About 4500 years ago people discovered how to make things from metal. This discovery changed many parts of life. What were these changes? How were people's lives different from in the Stone Age?

Bronze Age   Iron Age
hill fort
roundhouse

The Stone Age
c12000 BCE–2500 BCE

The Bronze Age
c3800 BCE–1200 BCE

The Iron Age
c1200 BCE–43 CE

12 000 BCE

43 CE

2 The Metal Ages

19

2.1 Technology in the Bronze Age

The Bronze Age began when people created a new material called bronze. People started using bronze instead of stone to make tools, weapons and other objects. Why was bronze better than stone? How did bronze change farming? How did bronze change other parts of life?

What is bronze?

People discovered a metal called copper and they used it to make tools and weapons. They also knew about another metal called tin. They mixed copper and tin together to create a new material called bronze. Bronze is much harder than either copper or tin.

Bronze Age people dug mines to reach the copper and tin ore. They broke up the ores and heated them together until the metals melted and mixed together. They poured the liquid bronze into moulds to make different objects.

Glossary words

mould
ore
plough
scythe

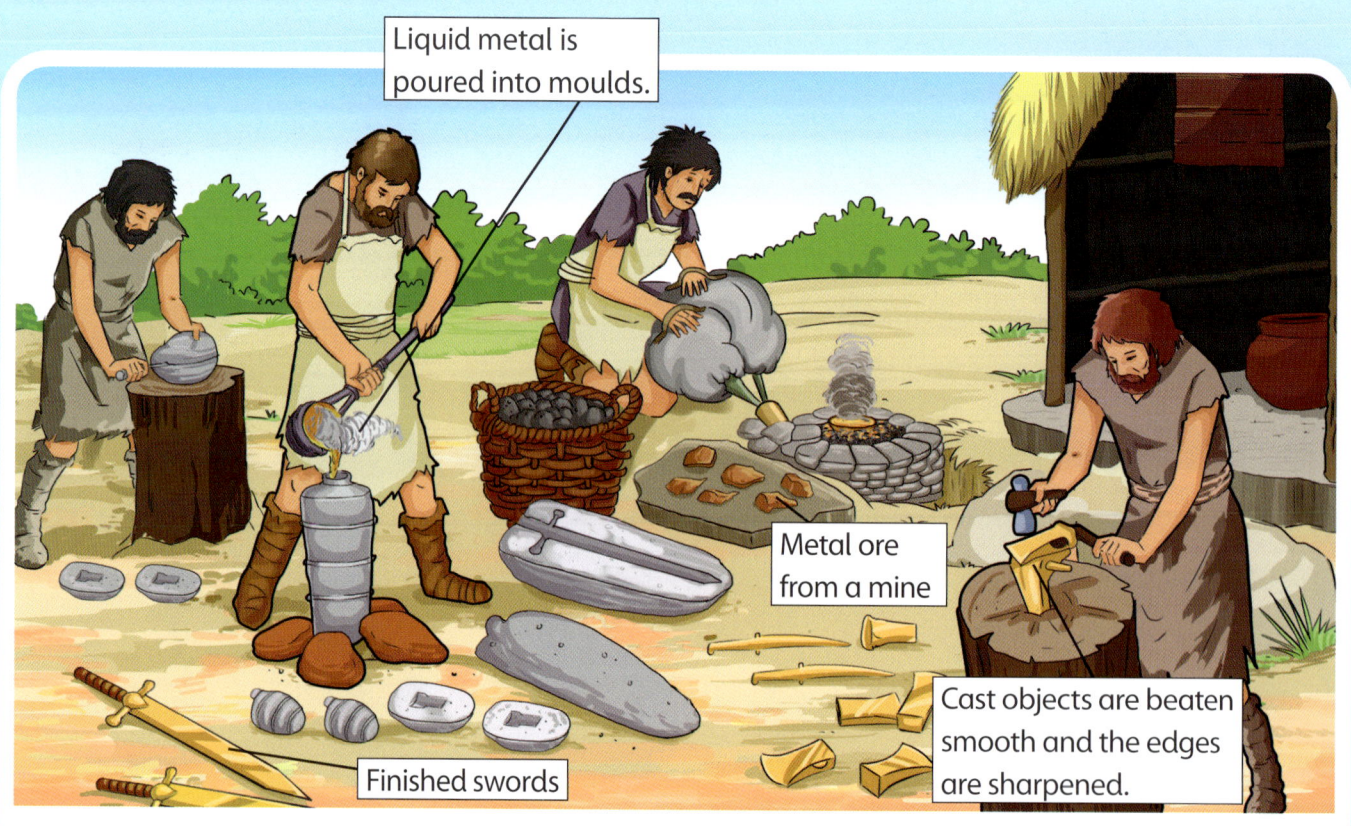

Liquid metal is poured into moulds.

Metal ore from a mine

Cast objects are beaten smooth and the edges are sharpened.

Finished swords

Casting bronze in moulds meant that people could make a greater range of tools and weapons.

20

Farming technology

Bronze was used to make the blades on ploughs. Bronze ploughs could cut through heavier soil than wooden ploughs.

Bronze axes helped clear forests to create more farming land.

The blades of bronze knives and scythes were sharper than stone blades. These bronze tools helped with harvesting crops.

The potter's wheel was invented. The potter's wheel made it much easier and faster to make pottery. People needed pottery containers for storing, carrying and cooking food.

The potter's wheel soon led to the idea of using wheels on carts.

Farms produced more food than before and so the farms could feed more people.

The Bronze Age around the world

Bronze-making was discovered in the Middle East in about 3800 BCE. People with bronze-making skills first arrived in Britain in about 2500 BCE.

Archeologists do not find the remains of Bronze Age wheels very often. This wooden wheel is 3000 years old. It was found in Cambridgeshire, England.

Archeologists think that a group of people known as the Beaker people took bronze-making skills to Britain from Europe. They are called Beaker people because of the style of pottery they made. This pot was made in about 3000 BCE.

Activities

1 Work in a group.
  a Make a list of Bronze Age objects for use in a home or on a farm.
  b For each object, write one reason why bronze is a better material for this object than stone or wood.
2 Use books or the Internet to find out about objects from the Bronze Age found in your country. Write a short report.

Challenge

Use books and the Internet to find out if there have ever been tin or copper mines in your country. If not, where is the nearest place with a tin or copper mine?

2.2 Towns, trade and travel

Farming improved during the Bronze Age. More food could be grown by fewer people. This allowed some people to do other work. Some people lived in new settlements. People began to travel further. What other work did people do? What new settlements did they build? Where and why did people travel?

Where were the first cities?

In Neolithic times, most people lived in small villages surrounded by farmland. When people started using bronze, a new way of living developed. For the first time, people began to live in large cities.

Some early cities were built near rivers. Rivers provided water and fish. People also used the rivers for transporting goods and travelling between places. Some cities were built on high ground. From the high ground it was easier to see an enemy coming. The city was also easier to defend.

Ruins of ancient cities built of mud brick provide evidence of life in the Bronze Age. These city walls were built about 3800 years ago.

Some people lived in cities because they felt safer there. Other people lived in cities because there was work.

Bronze Age working life

New jobs developed throughout the Bronze Age. People worked as builders of cities and houses. People worked as miners in tin and copper mines. Metal-workers, weavers and potters made things that other people needed. Traders brought food and other goods from the countryside into the cities.

Glossary words

goods
society
trade

Trade

Trade took place between the city and the countryside. Cities also traded with each other. Some goods were traded with different countries.

Transport

Trade led to developments in transport. People developed wheeled vehicles pulled by animals. These vehicles travelled along new roads and tracks that joined different places. Some goods travelled by boat. Boats became larger and stronger than before.

Leaders and organisers

Small Bronze Age cities had a few thousand people living in them. Some of the largest cities may have had as many as 100 000 people. Large cities needed people to lead and organise society.

Traded items included almonds (1), grapes (2), timber (3), glass (4), tin (5) and grains (6), as well as other goods such as copper, gold and silver jewellery, olives and figs.

This model of a wheeled cart was made in Mesopotamia between 2400 and 2000 BCE.

Activities

1. Work in a group. Prepare a presentation to convince a Bronze Age tribe that you know the best place to build a city.

2. You have found some Bronze Age objects. These include a scythe, some gold jewellery, glass beads, a clay pot and a model of a cart. Explain what each object tells us about life and work in the Bronze Age.

Challenge

Find out about one material or product that was traded between two different countries during the Bronze Age.

2.3 Life and death in the Iron Age

In about 800 BCE people learned how to use iron. The new iron tools made many parts of daily life easier than before. What work did people do during the Iron Age? What happened when people died?

What was the advantage of iron?

Bronze was made using tin. Tin was not easy to find so it was expensive. Bronze was mostly used by important people and for important things. Iron was easier to find than bronze and so iron was cheaper. Almost everyone could afford to have objects made from iron.

It was difficult to make objects from bronze. Metal-workers had to pour the bronze into moulds. Iron was easier to work with. Metal-workers could heat the iron and then beat it into shape.

Iron had other advantages. Iron weapons and armour were stronger than bronze weapons. Armies using iron weapons won battles more easily. Iron farm tools were stronger than other tools. Farmers who used iron tools could farm more land and produce more food.

Work

Most people in the **Iron Age** still worked as farmers producing food. People also had many other tasks to do. Iron Age people developed tools, such as the rotary quern and the loom, to make these tasks easier and faster.

The rotary quern is made of one flat, round stone on top of another stone. It is used to grind grain to make flour.

The rotary quern and loom were important developments in the Early Iron Age.

Death and burial

Archeologists have found many Iron Age burial sites. In some places people were buried with objects such as pots, mirrors, jewellery and swords. These objects show us the things people owned during their lifetime. They also tell us about the society. Important people had more expensive things buried with them.

What do objects like these tell us about the Iron Age?

Be a good historian

A good historian looks for similarities and differences between different periods of time such as the Stone Age, the Bronze Age and the Iron Age. Can you think of any similarities and differences between these periods of time?

Activities

1 Work in a group. Find out about some Iron Age tools. Create a class display with:

   a drawings of the tools

   b brief descriptions of how the tools worked

   c brief explanations of how the tools changed people's lives.

2 Imagine you are an archeologist. You have found some objects in the remains of an Iron Age house. Write what you think each object tells you about the people who lived in the house:

   a a mirror of polished metal

   b a large decorated shield

   c the remains of a loom.

Challenge

Find out about Iron Age musical instruments. Are there any in a museum near you? What do objects like these tell us about life in the Iron Age?

2.4 Iron Age settlements

There were many different groups of people in the Iron Age. Large groups often lived together in settlements. How were these groups organised? What were the settlements like?

Iron Age tribal kingdoms

People formed groups or clans and belonged to tribes. Different tribes fought over land and stole things such as cattle from each other. Each tribe had a powerful chief. The tribal chief had many responsibilities. They led and organised the tribe. They defended the tribe's land and trained their people to fight other tribes. They made sure that people followed the rules of the tribe.

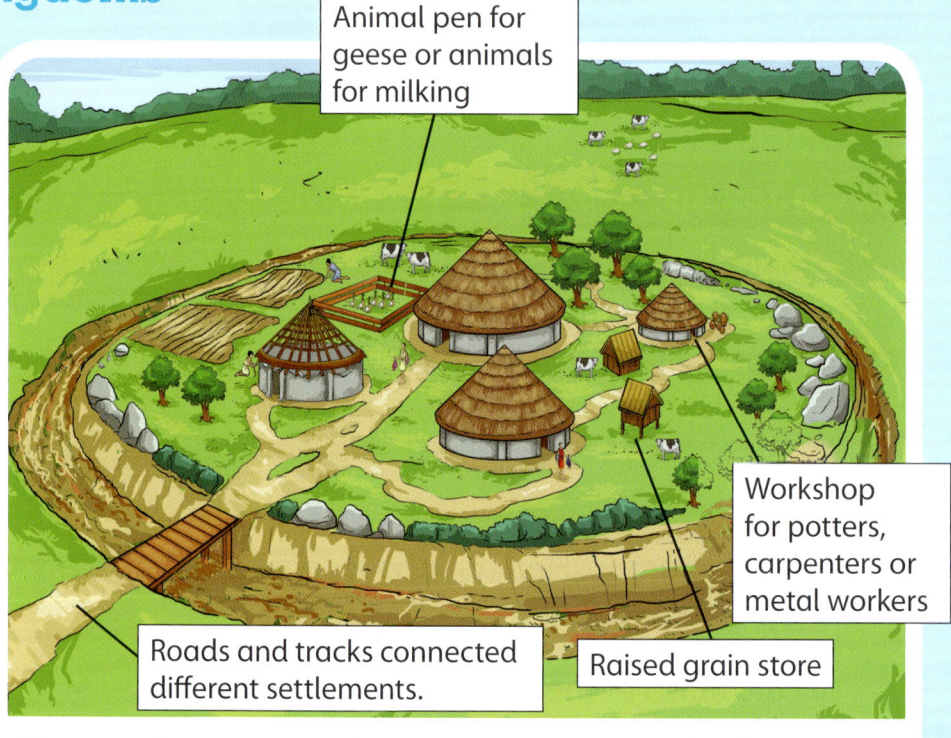

Animal pen for geese or animals for milking

Workshop for potters, carpenters or metal workers

Roads and tracks connected different settlements.

Raised grain store

Many settlements were home to just one extended family.

An Iron Age village

Most people still lived in the countryside. Settlements often had just a few homes surrounded by fields.

Most people worked on the land. Men ploughed the fields and went hunting or fishing. In some places they dug peat for fuel. The most important special job was metal-working.

Women prepared food. They stored enough food for the winter months when nothing grew. Women milked cows or goats, made cheese and prepared dried fish and meat. They ground grain to make bread and porridge. Many women were skilled at making pottery and weaving clothes.

Glossary words

clan   stable
peat   tribe

Children helped with jobs around the house and the farm. They cleaned, collected firewood and water, collected berries and spread manure on the fields. They looked after the animals and cleaned the stables.

Everyone spent a lot of time harvesting crops.

Iron Age roundhouse

In many countries in Europe people built **roundhouses**. The roundhouses were made from local materials. People chose the round shape because it was very strong.

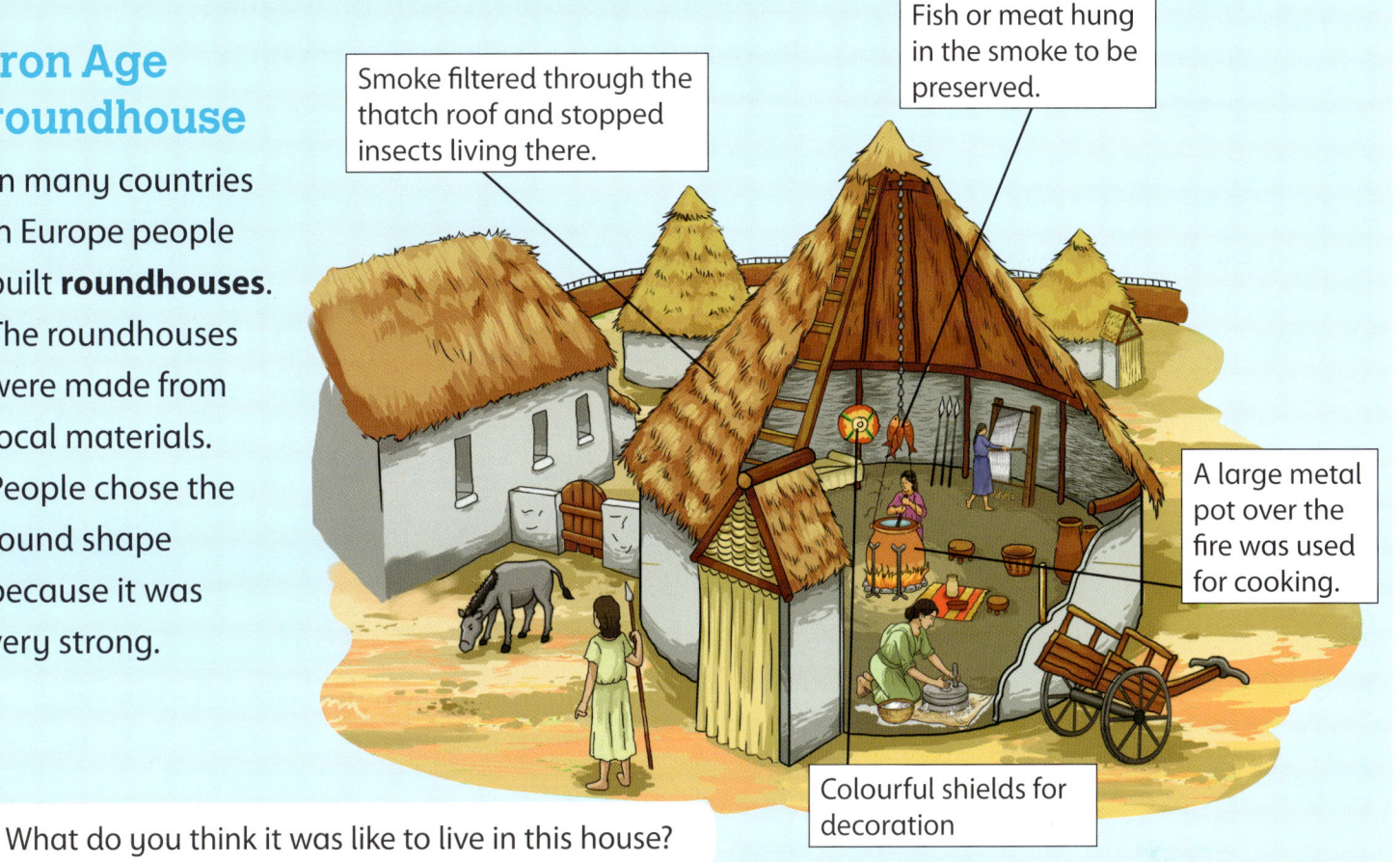

Smoke filtered through the thatch roof and stopped insects living there.

Fish or meat hung in the smoke to be preserved.

A large metal pot over the fire was used for cooking.

Colourful shields for decoration

What do you think it was like to live in this house?

Activities

1. Work in a group. Take turns to describe one task carried out by a man, woman or child in an Iron Age village. Score one point for each task you name. Miss a go if you cannot name a task.
2. Work in a group. Find out about Iron Age settlements in your country. Create a large poster to show the information.

Challenge

Find out about an Iron Age object called a torc. Draw a labelled diagram of a torc. Write about what the torc is made from and who may have worn it.

2.5 Fighting tribes or traders?

The Iron Age was a violent time for many people. It was also a time when trade was important. Where could people find safety? Which goods were traded?

Iron Age warriors

Most Iron Age warriors were well-trained men. Sometimes everyone had to fight, including women.

Most warriors carried a sword and a shield. Many warriors were tall. Some wore helmets to make them seem even taller. Some formed their hair into spikes and dyed it white.

Before a battle, warriors shouted and screamed. They banged their swords and shields. Some warriors blew horns. They made all this noise to scare their enemy.

Some warriors rode on horseback, others rode in chariots.

Charging Iron Age warriors wanted to look as terrifying as possible.

Hill forts

Some tribes built **hill forts**. These were areas of high ground with walls and ditches built around them.

Some people lived permanently inside a hill fort. Tribespeople from surrounding villages moved into the hill fort if they were attacked.

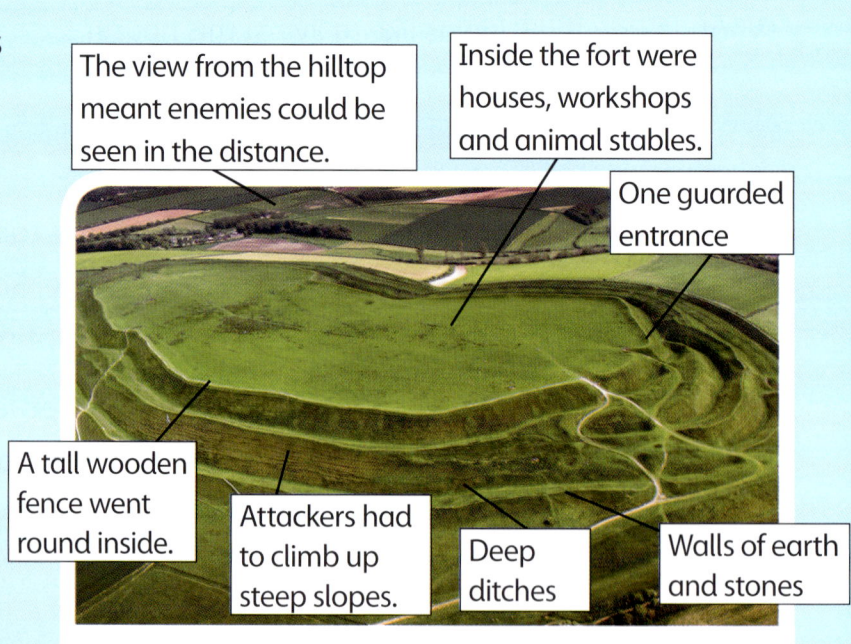

- The view from the hilltop meant enemies could be seen in the distance.
- Inside the fort were houses, workshops and animal stables.
- One guarded entrance
- A tall wooden fence went round inside.
- Attackers had to climb up steep slopes.
- Deep ditches
- Walls of earth and stones

The remains of Iron Age hill forts can still be seen. This is Maiden Castle in Dorset, England. It was built in about 600 BCE and expanded in 450 BCE.

Trade

Trade happened within a country and between different countries. People exchanged goods until they started using coins, at the end of the Iron Age. Then people bought and sold goods for money.

Items that people traded worldwide included:

- basic goods such as tin, copper, salt
- foods including grains and olive oil
- precious goods such as incense, silk and spices
- manufactured goods such as textiles, glass beads, jewellery and special pottery.

The end of the Iron Age

The Iron Age in Europe ended when the Romans invaded. Caesar invaded Gaul (the name given to a large part of Western Europe during the Iron Age) in 51 BCE and Britain in 43 CE. Iron Age life carried on in areas not conquered by the Romans.

Glossary words

chariot   dyed   incense

The Phoenicians were an ancient people who settled on the eastern Mediterranean. They became expert shipbuilders and traded with many different countries.

Activities

1. Imagine you have survived a battle against warriors from an Iron Age tribe. Write a report describing what you saw and heard before the battle began.

2. Use the information in this book and further research to find out about three goods that people traded during the Iron Age. Draw each item. Make a class display. On a world map, place your drawing of each item in the country it came from.

Did you know?

Some Iron Age warriors tattooed their bodies with a blue plant dye called woad.

Challenge

Research the locations of three Iron Age hill forts in different countries.

2 The Metal Ages

29

2 Review

Answer these questions in your notebook.

Choose the best answer from the choices below. Write a, b or c as your answer.

1. The Bronze Age ended when people began to use:
   a copper
   b iron
   c tin

2. In some places, during the Bronze Age, people lived together in very large settlements called:
   a villages
   b farms
   c cities

3. People started to use iron instead of bronze because iron was:
   a cheaper and stronger
   b stronger and more expensive
   c softer and cheaper

4. Archeologists have found a gold bracelet, a decorated sword and a shield in an Iron Age burial site. These objects tell us that the person buried there was:
   a a farmer
   b a warrior chief
   c a trader

5. Most people in Europe in the Iron Age lived in:
   a small farming settlements
   b hill forts
   c castles

6. Some Iron Age warriors rode into battle in a two-wheeled vehicle called a:
   a wagon
   b cart
   c chariot

Decide if these statements are true or false. Write 'True' or 'False' for each one.

7. Iron plough blades helped farmers to farm more land.
8. Bronze Age settlements were built by rivers so the people could be safe.
9. Iron Age tribes did not fight against other tribes.
10. Iron Age people used local materials to build their roundhouses.

11 Trade in tin was important during the Bronze Age.
12 People started using coins at the end of the Iron Age.

Now complete these tasks.

13 Imagine you are an archeologist and have found these objects. How do you think Bronze Age people used these objects to make swords? Write a description of the method they used.

14 Describe three features of an Iron Age hill fort that helped people to defend the fort from an attack.

15 This pot was made by people from the 'Beaker culture'. The same style of pottery is found in lots of different places. Some of these places are very far apart. Give one reason why pottery made by the Beaker people is found in all these different places.

3 Early civilisations

In this unit you will:
- describe some inventions from early civilisations
- talk about how people lived in early civilisations
- discuss similarities and differences between life in early civilisations
- describe some evidence that helps us know about early civilisations

Minoan

Tigris

Euphrates

Ancient Sumer

Indus Valley

Indus

Ancient Egypt

Ancient Sumerian stone carving of a boat

Figure of a bull from the Indus Valley civilisation

32

Life changed completely when people learned to make tools and weapons from bronze. In some places people started living and working together in large, organised groups. These groups are called **civilisations**. Where were these first civilisations located? When did they first appear?

civilisation
society

? The artefacts shown on this page come from three different early civilisations. What do these artefacts tell us about life in these civilisations?

A bronze jug from the Shang Dynasty

Yellow River

Shang Dynasty

Ancient Sumer
c3500 BCE –2400 BCE

Indus Valley
c2600 BCE–1700 BCE

Shang Dynasty
c1600 BCE–1046 BCE

4000 BCE

1000 BCE

3 Early civilisations

33

3.1 Early civilisations

Historians say a civilisation is a type of advanced society. In a civilisation many people live in large settlements. As well as farming, some people have other jobs to do. A small group of people organise and control people's lives. Some people are more important than others. Where were the first civilisations? Why did they develop? How do they compare?

Glossary words

city-state
dynasty
fertile
government

Early civilisations

Three early civilisations developed near rivers. The land near the rivers was fertile. Most people were farmers who could grow plenty of food. The safe supply of food allowed the civilisations to develop.

Some things were similar in all these civilisations. They all had:

- larger permanent settlements
- a form of writing
- new technology
- a special style of art.

Ancient Sumer

In about 5000 BCE the first people in Sumer lived in small villages. By about 3600 BCE more people lived in larger towns. Each town became a city-state with its own ruler and government.

The Indus Valley

Farmers settled in the Indus Valley in about 4000 BCE. The first cities appeared in about 3000 BCE. There were many towns by 2600 BCE. Experts are not sure how **society** in the Indus Valley was organised.

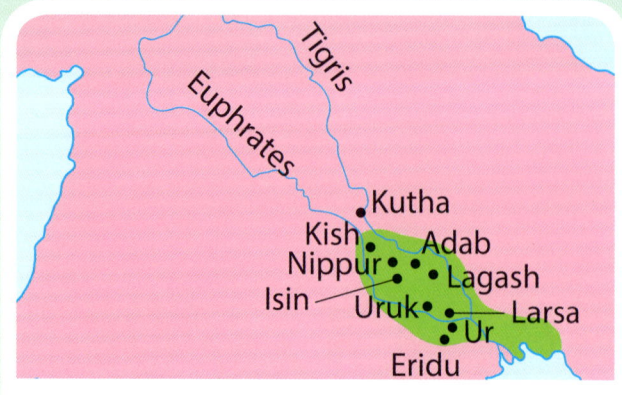

The earliest civilisation in the world developed in Sumer. This was in a part of the world that is now southern Iraq.

The Indus Valley civilisation developed around cities on the Indus River. This is in modern-day Pakistan and northern India.

The Shang Dynasty civilisation

The Shang Dynasty began in about 1600 BCE. Archeologists have found remains of many cities from this time. The first king of the Shang Dynasty was Cheng Tang.

The Shang Dynasty civilisation was based around the Yellow River in part of China.

Timeline of early civilisations

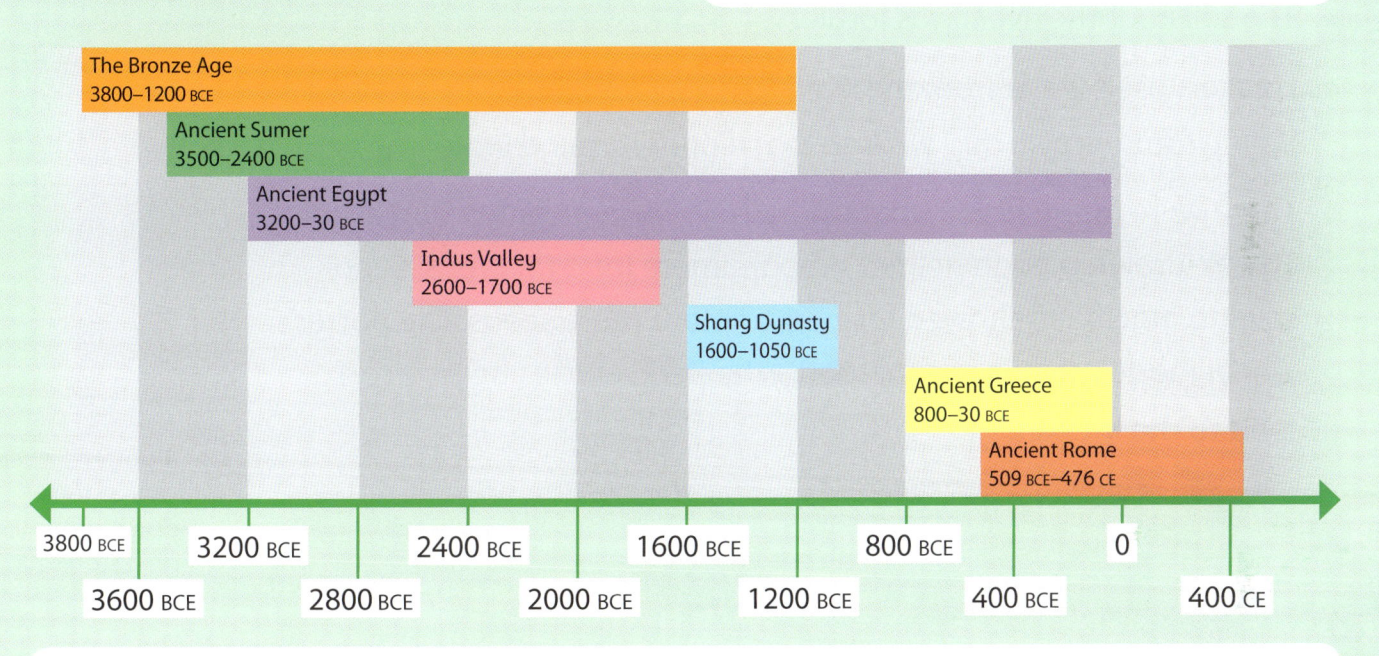

- The Bronze Age 3800–1200 BCE
- Ancient Sumer 3500–2400 BCE
- Ancient Egypt 3200–30 BCE
- Indus Valley 2600–1700 BCE
- Shang Dynasty 1600–1050 BCE
- Ancient Greece 800–30 BCE
- Ancient Rome 509 BCE–476 CE

The timeline shows that early civilisations began when people developed the use of bronze.

Activities

1. Work in a group to make a presentation. Explain briefly how and why early civilisations developed.
2. Use the timeline and your mathematical skills to work out how long each civilisation lasted.

Challenge

Research the climate where the earliest civilisations were located. How did the climate influence people's clothes and food?

3.2 Farming and food

Farming was very important in all early civilisations. How did the farmers grow so much food? What food did they grow? Why was it important for farmers to know the different times of year?

Farming

Three important things helped farmers in early civilisations.

- The soil near the rivers was fertile.

- Farmers used water from the rivers to water their crops. In the Indus Valley farmers also dug wells to reach underground water.

- There were many new inventions to help farmers grow more food. The ox-drawn plough helped prepare more land for crops. Seed-sowing machines allowed farmers to plant more seeds. The potter's wheel made storage jars for food. Wheeled vehicles helped carry food to the market.

A A potter's wheel was a stone disc that turned on a stone base.

B The potter's wheel led to the idea of wheeled vehicles.

C Ploughs pulled by animals made ploughing easier and faster.

D People dug channels to bring water from the river to the fields.

E A shaduf was a machine for raising water from the channels onto the fields.

Farming in Ancient Sumer

36

Farming and the calendar

Many early civilisations developed calendars. These calendars helped farmers. The farmers needed to know:

- weather conditions at different times of year
- when to plant crops
- when the rivers might flood.

Calendars in the Sumerian and Indus Valley civilisations divided years into 12 months. Months were based on the cycles of the moon. Each month had 29 or 30 days. There were no weeks in the calendar.

The Shang Dynasty calendar was based on a period of 60 days. This was divided into 6 periods of 10 days.

What did people eat?

People in early civilisations ate the food produced by farmers. Basic foods included grains such as wheat, barley, millet and rice. Sheep, goats and cows provided milk. Chickens and wild birds provided eggs and meat. People also ate fish and shellfish. Most people ate very little meat.

What did people wear?

In Sumer and the Indus Valley, people wore clothes made from the fibres of local plants and the wool from sheep or goats. In the Shang Dynasty, rich people may have worn silk.

Glossary word

silk

Activities

1 Research an invention from one of the early civilisations you are studying. Prepare a presentation that:

   a describes the invention

   b explains what it does

   c describes why the invention will be useful.

2 Work in a group to create a poster of the clothes a family in an ancient civilisation might wear.

Challenge

Find out about the foods people ate in an early civilisation. Write about how these are the same as or different from the foods you eat today.

3.3 City life in the early civilisations

There were many jobs to do in ancient civilisations. Some people worked on building projects. Other people learned new skills such as pottery, metal-working and weaving. There were different groups of people within each civilisation. What did people build? What did people make? Which different groups were people in?

What were the first cities like?

Cities were a new development in the early civilisations. These cities were carefully planned. The streets were laid out in a grid pattern. Buildings included houses, shops, workshops, markets, palaces and gardens.

People in the Sumerian and Indus Valley civilisations used mud bricks to build their houses and cities. People in the Shang Dynasty civilisation made a solid floor of gravel, sand and mud. On top, they built a wooden frame with a thatch roof.

Glossary words

labourer
scribe
thatch

Groups within society

People in the Sumerian and Shang civilisations were grouped in a similar way. There were a few rich and powerful people at the top of society. There were groups of people in the middle level who had certain skills. Then there were large numbers of farmers, labourers and slaves.

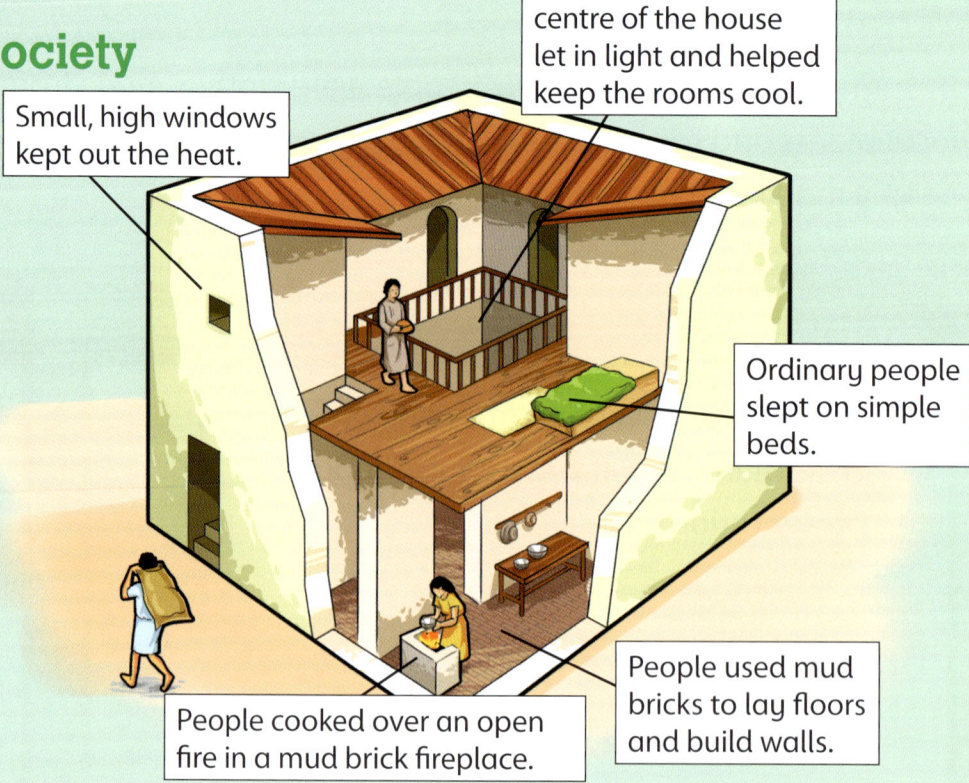

- Small, high windows kept out the heat.
- A courtyard in the centre of the house let in light and helped keep the rooms cool.
- Ordinary people slept on simple beds.
- People cooked over an open fire in a mud brick fireplace.
- People used mud bricks to lay floors and build walls.

The houses in Sumerian cities may have looked like this one. Compare this house with the house from the Indus Valley.

House were built close together.

Food was left on the flat roof to dry in the sun.

Ordinary people slept on simple beds.

Walls of mud or mud plaster

Thatch roof

Some houses had a well inside.

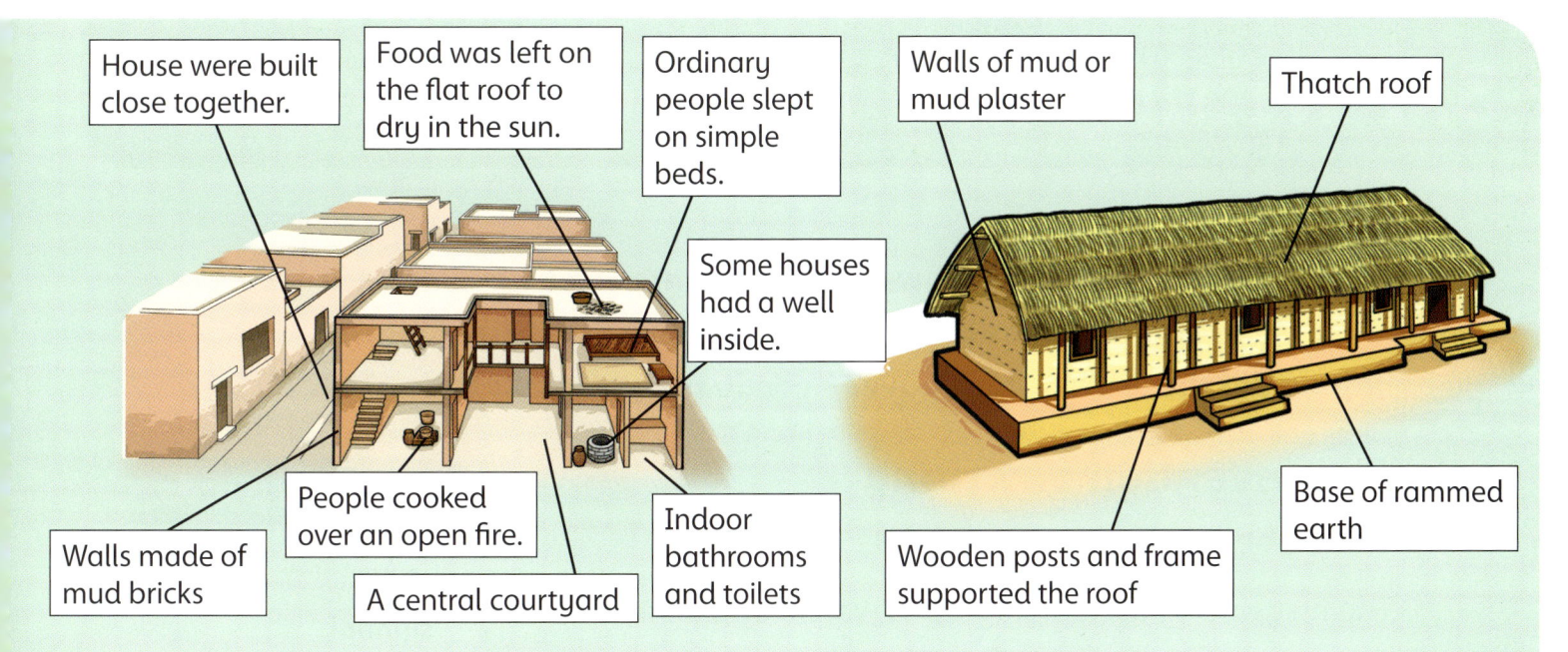

Walls made of mud bricks

People cooked over an open fire.

A central courtyard

Indoor bathrooms and toilets

Wooden posts and frame supported the roof

Base of rammed earth

Houses of wealthy families in an Indus Valley city may have looked like this. Many poorer people lived in houses with only one room.

A village house from the Shang Dynasty civilisation

In the Indus Valley, some houses were bigger than others. This is a clue that some people were wealthy and others were poor.

Did you know?

At one time, the two largest cities in the Indus Valley each had about 40 000 people living in them.

Working life

Being able to read and write was important in early civilisations. People who could read and write were called scribes. Working as a scribe was a good job to have.

There were many craftspeople. They worked making pottery, furniture, tools, clothes and jewellery.

Activities

1. Work in a group to draw a plan of a city for an early civilisation. Show the layout of streets and include houses, shops, workshops, a market, schools and other important buildings.

2. Role play a job from an early civilisation. Other students have to guess your job.

Challenge

Find out how people in an ancient civilisation made mud bricks.

3.4 Writing and number systems

Writing and number systems were both invented and developed in early civilisations. What did writing and numbers look like? What impact did these inventions have? How do they affect us today?

The invention of writing

Writing began in Sumer in about 3200 BCE.

The first writing used pictographs which represented different objects or ideas. Over time the pictographs became simpler.

Glossary words

stylus   tax
symbol

In Sumer the pictographs eventually became a kind of writing called cuneiform. Scribes used a stylus made of reed, wood or bone to press wedge shapes into tablets of wet clay. They then left the clay to dry.

Sumerian pictographs from 3200 BCE	hand	barley	water
Indus Valley pictographs from about 2000 BCE	?	?	?
Shang Dynasty symbols 1500–1000 BCE	horse	cart	fish

Writing from the Indus Valley civilisation used at least 400 pictographs.

Symbols from early writing systems. What do you think the symbols from the Indus Valley civilisation mean?

In Shang Dynasty writing each symbol was a separate word.

Why did people write?

Most writing from early Sumer is about business and government. There are some stories and teaching texts. People also used writing to record laws. The Code of Ur-Nammu is the earliest example of written laws. It is written on clay tablets dating from about 2100 BCE.

No-one today can understand the Indus Valley writing.

Writing from the Shang Dynasty was scratched into turtle shells and animal bones. This writing was used in special ceremonies.

Number systems

People in all early civilisations developed number systems and mathematics. They needed to measure and record:

- the boundaries of a field (length)
- numbers of objects (counting)
- amounts of liquid or grain (volume)
- taxes (counting)
- dimensions of objects such as bricks (length)
- value of goods (weight).

Mathematics in the Shang Dynasty was mostly used to record the movement of stars and planets.

Did you know?

Our number system is based on 10, but the number system in Sumer was based on 60. The Sumerian number system gives us our 60 seconds in a minute, 60 minutes in an hour and the 360 degrees in a circle.

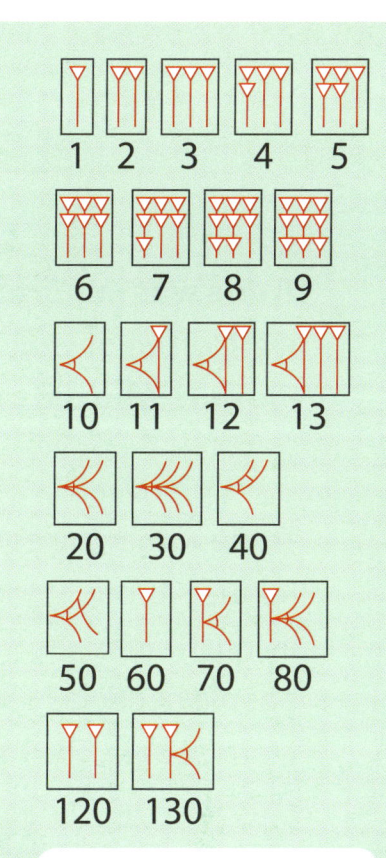

Symbols from the Sumerian number system

Activities

1. Make up some pictographs. Use them to write a simple message. Swap your message with a partner. Can you understand each other's messages?

2. Work with a partner. Write three things that people in an early civilisation needed to:

   a measure to find the length

   b weigh

   c count.

Challenge

Numbers and writing changed life in early civilisations. People could now measure and record things. Create a poster that explains some of the things that changed because of numbers and writing.

Precious items such as gem stones had to be weighed carefully. A small change in weight could make a big difference in value.

3 Early civilisations

3.5 Trade and war

Trade was important in early civilisations. Different groups of people were often at war. Which goods were traded? How were goods moved? Why did different groups go to war?

Trading peoples

Trade within the early civilisations was important. Farmers brought food from the countryside to people living in cities. Craftspeople made things that other people needed. Merchants brought materials for the craftspeople. The merchants took away the objects the craftspeople made.

Objects from the Indus Valley have been found in the region of Sumer and in countries of the Arabian Gulf.

Some of the items that people traded are shown on the map. Other traded items included exotic foods and animals, ivory and oils. These early civilisations traded grains, oils and textiles in exchange for stone, hard timber and metal.

In the Shang Dynasty people mostly traded between themselves. Cities inland traded with ports on the coast. Items traded included bronze containers, jewellery, silk cloth and weapons.

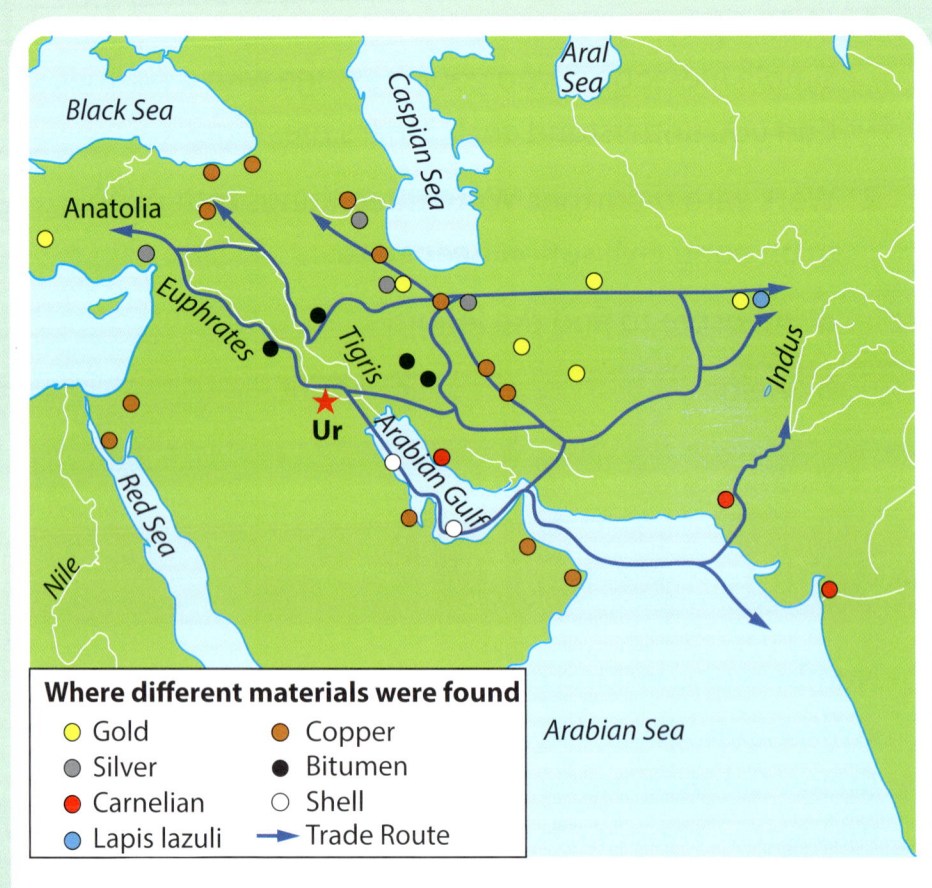

Glossary words

bitumen
port

Where different materials were found
- Gold
- Silver
- Carnelian
- Lapis lazuli
- Copper
- Bitumen
- Shell
- → Trade Route

Trade routes of the early Sumer and Indus Valley civilisations

Transportation

People or pack animals carried small items. Ox-drawn carts transported larger loads. The largest loads went by barge along the river or across the sea on sail boats.

War

The city-states in Sumer often fought each other over farmland. They also wanted to control trade on the rivers.

Shang Dynasty rulers had large armies to defend their territory. The civilisation ended when it was beaten by a rival dynasty, the Zhou, in 1046 BCE.

The people of the Indus Valley civilisation seem to have been very peaceful. There is little evidence of war such as weapons or armour.

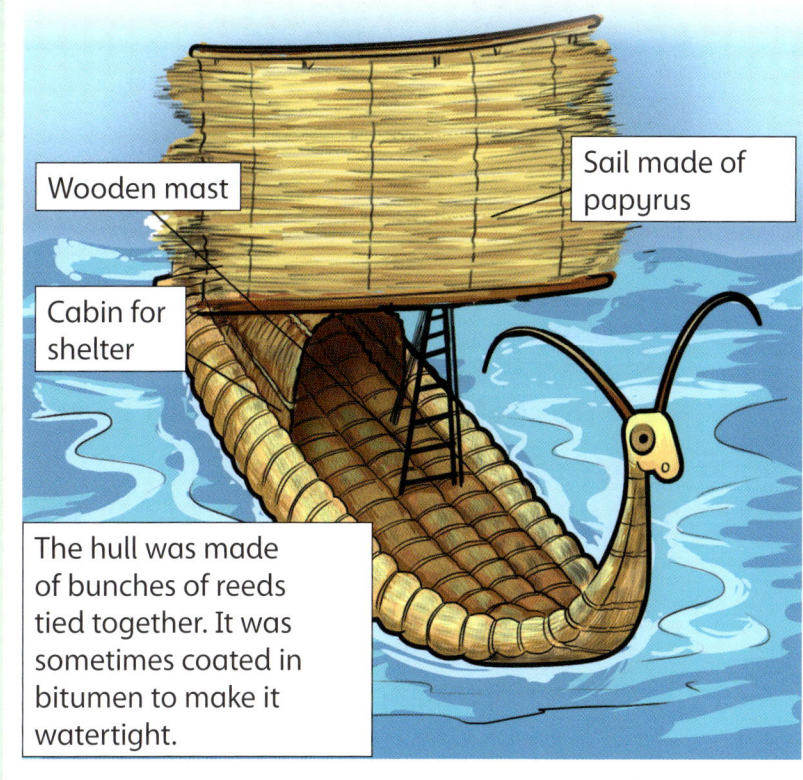

Wooden mast

Sail made of papyrus

Cabin for shelter

The hull was made of bunches of reeds tied together. It was sometimes coated in bitumen to make it watertight.

People made reed sail boats in the region of Sumer at least 6000 years ago.

Helmet of leather or bronze

Bow

Arrows

Dagger

Battle axe

The rulers of the Shang Dynasty were often at war with neighbouring regions and had large armies of soldiers.

Activities

1. Make up a role play between a Sumerian trader and a trader from the Indus Valley. Discuss the items you have to trade.
2. In a group, draw a map of a Sumerian city-state. Add labels to show what is valuable and why the city-state might be attacked.

Challenge

Find out about barges and ships from Sumer or the Indus Valley. Create a poster to show how these boats were made and how they carried goods.

3 Review

Answer these questions in your notebook.

Choose the best answer from the choices below. Write a, b or c as your answer.

1. Early civilisations developed during the:
   a Stone Age
   b Iron Age
   c Bronze Age
2. A city-state is:
   a a collection of small villages
   b a city and the surrounding lands
   c a town built near a river
3. The Shang Dynasty civilisation was based along the:
   a Green River
   b Yellow River
   c Blue River
4. Buildings in the Sumerian and Indus Valley civilisations were made from:
   a mud bricks
   b rammed earth
   c stone blocks
5. People living in the Indus Valley civilisation sometimes collected water from:
   a dams
   b wells
   c drains
6. Most people in early civilisations worked as:
   a scribes
   b jewellery-makers
   c farmers

7. This clay tablet has writing from Ancient Sumer. This writing is called:
   a curlicue
   b cuneiform
   c circular

Decide if these statements are true or false. Write 'True' or 'False' for each one.

8. A stylus is an ancient writing tool for making marks in clay.
9. Lapis lazuli and carnelian were important trade items. They are both precious metals.

10. People in all early civilisations developed number systems and mathematics to measure and record things such as the boundaries of a field and amounts of liquid or grain.

11. Linen was a soft luxury cloth that was an important trade item in the Shang Dynasty civilisation.

12. People in the Sumerian and Shang Dynasty civilisations often fought among themselves to control land and trade. The Indus Valley civilisation was more peaceful.

Now complete these tasks.

13. Write a brief explanation of why and how early civilisations developed. Include why soil, food, water supply and rivers were important.

14. Many stone carvings from the region of Ancient Sumer have been found. Write about what the image below tells us about water transport and trade.

15. This bronze object comes from the Shang Dynasty. It has a lot of detail. Write about what this object tells us about craftspeople at that time. What does an expensive object like this tell us about Shang Dynasty society?

4 A history of communication

In this unit you will:

- explore how different forms of communication have changed over time
- explain how different forms of historical evidence are used
- examine significant people and events in the history of communication
- analyse and describe important changes in communication and their effects

About 3200 BCE	About 2300 BCE	105 CE	1041–1048 CE	Mid-1400s	1840
The first cuneiform writing developed	The Egyptians created papyrus	Cai Lun invented paper in China	Bi Sheng invented moveable type in China	Gutenberg invented his printing press	First postage stamp, the Penny Black

People have always communicated. This means they have shared information, stories, ideas and feelings.
Communication happens when people speak and write. What are all the different ways in which communication takes place? How have the ways in which people communicate changed over time? What effects have these changes had?

invention   printing
postal service
communication
satellite

? Look at the different methods of communication on this page. Can you name each method? These methods of communication are from different times. Write the methods down in the order in which you think they were first used. Can you explain your ideas?

1876	1896	1925	1962	1989	1994
First telephone	First radio	First public demonstration of a television	First communications satellite	Tim Berners-Lee invented the World Wide Web	First smart phone

4 A history of communication

47

4.1 Writing and writing tools

Before writing, all language was spoken. Writing meant that people could store and share information in new ways. When was writing invented? How have the tools used for writing changed? What do we write with today?

The invention of writing

The first examples of early writing date from about 3200 BCE. Around the world, there are examples of early writing pressed into clay tablets and scratched into animal bones, shells and metal. Some early writing was on tree bark and specially-prepared animal skins. Some important writing was carved into stone. In about 2300 BCE, the Ancient Egyptians invented an early form of paper called papyrus.

Paper

True paper is made from plant and cloth fibres. A man called Cai Lun invented paper in China in about 105 CE.

Paper-making spread to India by the 7th century CE and the Islamic world in the 8th century CE. It reached Europe by the 11th century.

Pens and pencils

The Ancient Sumerian people wrote by pressing a stylus into clay tablets. The Ancient Egyptians wrote with reed brushes. By the 4th century BCE, the Egyptians developed reed pens. Reed pens were made from lengths of thin reed. The end was cut to form a point called a nib.

Over time, the quill pen replaced the reed pen. The quill pen was a large feather with a nib cut in the end. Quill pens were used in Europe from the 6th century CE.

Glossary words

century   stylus
graphite   tablet
papyrus

The earliest known writing system developed in the ancient civilisation of Sumer about 3200 BCE. This writing is called cuneiform, which means 'wedge-shaped'.

The Romans used pens with metal nibs in the 1st century CE. Metal nibs were first made in large quantities in the 1800s.

People had to dip a nib pen in ink before writing with the pen. The next development was the fountain pen. This held ink inside the pen. Modern fountain pens were first made in 1827.

In 1938, a Hungarian named László Bíró introduced his design for a ballpoint pen.

In the 1960s, Yukio Horie invented felt-tipped pens in Japan.

People have been using pencils that have a stick of graphite inside a wooden casing since about 1560.

Modern writing tools

Typewriters were developed in the 1860s.

Word processors and personal computers replaced typewriters in many places by the 1980s.

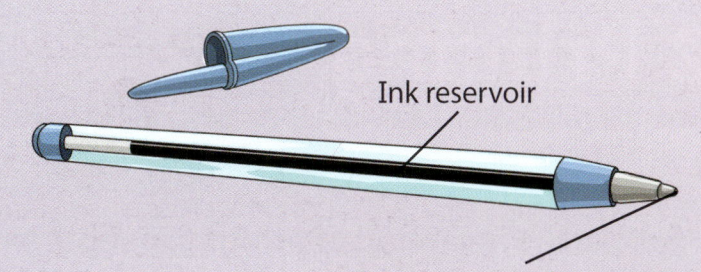

Ink reservoir

A ballpoint pen

Ballpoint pens have no nib. Instead there is a tiny ball that moves inside a socket in the tip of the pen.

Typewriters appeared in the 1860s. They quickly became the writing tool for professional writers, office workers and businesses.

Activities

1. Work in a group. Use the information in this book and further research to find out how writing began in Ancient Sumer, Ancient Egypt, the Indus Valley, Meso-America and China. Prepare a presentation to present your findings.

2. Write a description of a writing tool that was used in:
   a. Ancient Sumer
   b. the 12th century
   c. the 1950s.

Challenge

Carry out some research to find out how the method for making paper has changed over time.

4.2 Printing

Before the invention of printing, people wrote documents by hand. This method was very expensive and so only rich people and organisations could afford to produce documents. The invention of printing made it much cheaper to produce documents. When and where did printing begin? How did printing develop? What impact did it have?

The printing process

Printing is a process which produces the same image or text many times from one original. Printing lots of copies is much faster than copying documents by hand.

Wooden block printing

People in China used wooden blocks for printing in about 200 CE. They carved the image to be printed from a wooden block. Then they pressed cloth or paper onto the block to transfer the ink. Once the block was carved it could not be changed.

One printing block could print thousands of pages. Printing helped to spread knowledge and learning.

Moveable type

Between 1041 and 1048 CE, a Chinese man called Bi Sheng invented moveable type.

Bi Sheng made a small clay block for each Chinese character. The blocks were held in place inside a frame. He could change the order of the blocks to make new pieces of writing.

Wooden moveable type replaced clay moveable type in China in about 1297 CE. The first books printed using metal type were made in Korea in 1234 CE.

When using moveable type, the printer placed separate character blocks inside a frame.

Glossary word

moveable type

The printing press

In the mid-1400s a German man called Johannes Gutenberg invented a machine called a printing press. This new **invention** made printing faster and cheaper.

The impact of the printing press

Printing presses were soon used all over Europe. The printing press had three great effects. First, there were a lot more books, so more people learned to read. Second, information spread more quickly and accurately to more people. Third, scientists were able to print and share the results of their work. This helped them to improve their ideas and understanding. So printing changed people's knowledge and ideas about nature and the world.

Printing presses could print thousands of pages in a day. A printer using older methods probably printed about 40–50 pages a day.

Later printing presses

The design of printing presses did not change much until the 19th century. Presses were then made of iron and driven by steam.

Activities

1. How and why did the invention of the printing press lead to more learning?
2. Work in a group. Make a list of all the writing you see in a day. Do you read more in print or on a screen? How do you think we will access information in the future?

Challenge

Find out how modern printing presses work. Explain the similarities and differences between modern printing presses and printing presses from the past.

4.3 Staying in touch

Sending letters has been an important way of communicating for centuries. How did postal services begin? How have they changed? How else do we send messages today?

Where did early postal systems develop?

Early postal systems developed in many places, including Ancient Egypt, Persia, China, India, Central America, Greece and Rome. In most systems riders on horseback carried messages along a network of roads. The riders stopped at relay stations to collect fresh horses or to hand the messages on to new riders.

Glossary word

smart phone

Postal services grow

Over time, trade spread to more countries. Messenger services spread at the same time because merchants needed to communicate. After the invention of the printing press in the mid-1400s, more people learned to read and write. People wrote more letters, so delivering mail became an important business.

Where did the modern postal services begin?

Public **postal services** began in different European countries during the 17th and 18th centuries. Postal services in other places, such as the Americas and India, also improved during the 18th century.

Mail transport

Private horse-drawn mail coaches were introduced in Germany in 1650. John Palmer introduced mail coaches to England in 1784. The mail coaches were very fast and soon there were mail coach routes across England, Europe, America and Australia.

Old paintings show us how popular mail coaches were. This busy scene shows a street in North London in about 1820.

Ships called packet boats carried mail between countries in the 18th and 19th centuries. They carried mail around Europe and over the Atlantic Ocean to America.

Railways were built in many countries from the middle of the 1800s. Mail sent by rail arrived much faster than before. Railways became a major part of the postal system.

The airplane was invented in 1903 and a few years later airmail services began.

Paying for the post

In 1840, a man named Rowland Hill introduced the world's first postage stamp. The stamp shows that the person sending the letter has paid for postage. Stamps are still used all around the world.

What is electronic mail?

Today many people send messages using electronic mail (email). Email is a way of sending a message using a network of computers. People can send emails from their computers and smart phones.

People also communicate by sending text messages and using instant messaging services.

Mail is still carried by train in many parts of the world. Here postal workers unload sacks of mail from the train in Gujarat, India.

A Penny Black, the world's first stamp

Did you know?

An American computer scientist called Raymond Tomlinson sent the first email in 1971.

Activities

1 Work in a group. Find out how postal services in your country work today. Write about how the postal services have changed over time.

2 Discuss with a friend the advantages of email and of postal services.

Challenge

Use books and the Internet to research and write a brief report about the Pony Express in the USA.

4.4 Telecommunication

Telecommunication means exchanging information using technology. What was early telecommunication like? How have telephones changed over time? How do people use telecommunication today?

How can we send a message without a letter?

In the 1830s a number of people developed systems that used electricity to send messages down a wire. These systems are called telegraphs.

Telegraph messages used a special alphabet code, called Morse code. Morse code is made up of 'dots and dashes'. The person receiving the message understood the code and wrote the message in words on a telegram. A telegram messenger then delivered the telegram in the same way as a letter. The first telegraph was sent in the USA in 1838 across a distance of two miles.

1 Pressing the transmission key closes an electrical circuit.

2 A magnet here pulls a lever down towards the paper.

3 The pen tip marks dots and dashes on the paper.

A diagram showing how the telegraph works

Telegraph wires soon crossed whole countries. Eventually, telegraph cables were laid under the sea to connect different countries. People in the different countries could now be in direct contact with one another.

Telephones

Sending simple signals along wires was a big step forward in communication. The next step was to send the sound of the human voice. The device that allowed this to happen was the telephone.

A Scottish man called Alexander Graham Bell is said to have invented the first telephone in 1876. Bell was working in the USA, where he founded a telephone company in 1877.

Glossary word
radio

Telephones all work in a similar way. The sound of a person speaking is sent as a signal to another phone. The receiving phone turns the signal back into sound.

The first telephone networks connected people within a country. Then, from about 1890, telephone cables were laid to connect different countries. Telephone conversations were later sent using radio instead of wires. By the 1960s, signals were sent through space using communications **satellites**.

Mobile phones

The first call from a hand-held mobile phone was made on 3 April 1973. Mobile phones and networks quickly developed around the world. Mobile phones have been especially useful in countries that do not have a network of telephone wires.

There will probably be about 2.6 billion smart phone users in 2018. That is about one third of the world's population.

Telstar was the name of some early communications satellites. The first communications satellite went into space on a rocket in 1962. Telstar 1 relayed the first television pictures and telephone messages through space.

Activities

1. Work in a group. Prepare a presentation that shows when telephones were first used in your country and explains how the telephone system has changed.
2. Make a timeline that shows five major events in the history of telecommunications.

Did you know?

The first mobile telephone weighed 1.1 kilogram. It had a talk time of 30 minutes and took 10 hours to recharge.

Challenge

Find out what was said in the first messages sent by telephone and email.

4 A history of communication

55

4.5 Mass communication

Sharing information with many people at once is called mass communication. Forms of mass communication include newspapers, radio and television. Why did these forms of communication develop? How have they changed? What impact do they have?

Newspapers

In Ancient Rome (from 59 BCE) and in China (from about the 6th century CE), the governments posted daily messages in public spaces for people to read. This was an early form of daily news.

The earliest regular newspaper appeared in Europe in the 17th century. Newspapers were the only form of mass communication for hundreds of years.

Radio

In 1896, an Italian named Guglielmo Marconi registered his invention of the radio. Radio sends the energy from sound through the air. When a radio set receives the signal it turns the signal back into sound.

Radio became popular for entertainment, news and information by the 1920s.

In 1954, the portable transistor radio was introduced. The transistor radio was small and light and could be carried everywhere. It changed the way in which people listened to the radio.

Radio is still very popular today. Thousands of radio stations broadcast many different types of programme.

In the early 20th century, boys sold newspapers on the street. Newspapers informed people of major events from around the world.

In the 1920s, some families and friends gathered round the radio set to listen.

Glossary words

broadcast   online
newspaper   radio station

Television

In the late 1800s, several inventors were working on the idea of television. John Logie Baird was the first person to show transmitted television pictures. In 1925, he gave a public demonstration in a department store in London.

Television broadcasts began in Europe and the USA in the 1930s. By the 1950s, television programmes included sports, news, game shows, comedies and dramas. Television had become the new way for people to receive information.

In 1962, the first television signal via satellite was sent between England and the USA. Satellite television, which allows individual homes to receive a signal through a satellite dish, became popular in the 1990s.

The impact of the Internet

Many radio and television programmes are now transmitted over the Internet. Many newspapers now have an online edition.

The Internet allows anyone with a computer or smart phone to take part in mass communication. Anything a person uploads to mass communication websites or social media websites can be seen by millions around the world.

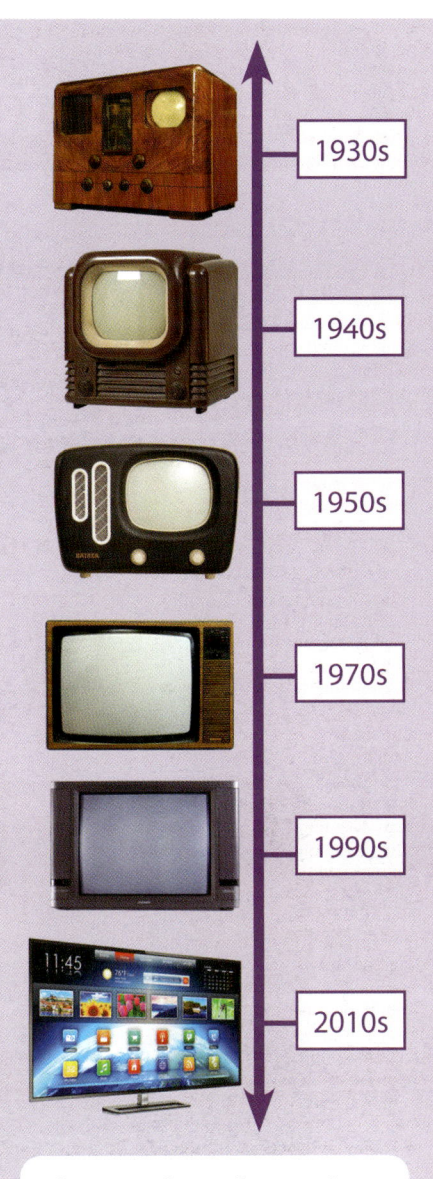

This timeline shows the advances in television design.

Activities

1 Work in a group. Find out when:
   a daily newspapers were first printed in your country
   b television broadcasts were first shown in your country.
2 Carry out a survey to find out how your family members access the news today. Create a pie chart to show your results.

Challenge

Draw a timeline showing at least six major events that have been broadcast on television since the 1930s.

4 Review

Answer these questions in your notebook.

Choose the best answer from the choices below. Write a, b or c as your answer.

1. The earliest known writing is about:
   a 520 years old
   b 5200 years old
   c 52 000 years old

2. The Ancient Egyptians made an early form of paper from:
   a sheep skin
   b fibres from the papyrus plant
   c wood pulp

3. Moveable type is a kind of printing that uses characters on:
   a a carved wooden block
   b soft rubber stamps
   c separate blocks that can be moved and rearranged

4. Johannes Gutenberg invented the printing press in about:
   a 1340
   b 1440
   c 1540

5. Paper was invented in:
   a Taiwan
   b Germany
   c China

6. The world's first postage stamp was called:
   a the Penny Black
   b the Penny Blue
   c the Penny Royal

7. Sending Morse code signals down a wire is called:
   a telephony
   b telegraphy
   c television

58

8 The person who invented the telephone was called:
   a John Logie Baird
   b Guglielmo Marconi
   c Alexander Graham Bell

Decide if these statements are true or false. Write 'True' or 'False' for your answer.

9 Telephones were invented 200 years ago.
10 The first public demonstration of television was in 1925.
11 The earliest regular newspaper appeared in Europe in the 15th century CE.

Now complete these tasks.

12 Write about how methods of sending personal messages have changed between Roman times and the present day.
13 Write about some of the changes that have happened to telephone services. Explain the main differences and similarities between old telephones and modern smart phones.     
14 Some historians compare the invention of the printing press to the invention of the Internet. Why do you think historians make this comparison?
15 Write a report that explains briefly how radio or television has changed since it was first introduced.

4 A history of communication

Vocabulary quiz

Answer these questions in your notebook.

1 From hunter-gatherers to village people

1 Match the words with the definitions.
 a a time in the past before people could write
 b objects made from clay and baked to become hard
 c a place where people live and make a community
 d people who move from one place to another instead of settling down
 e a tool with a blade for cutting down trees or chopping wood

> nomads   prehistoric   settlement
> axe   pottery

2 Write a definition for each of the following words. Then use each word correctly in a sentence or short paragraph.
 a hunter-gatherers
 b farmer
 c Stone Age
 d Bronze Age
 e plough

2 The Metal Ages

1 a Sort the words below in a table.

Groups of people	Farming tools	Household tools

> clan   loom   plough
> rotary quern   scythe   tribe

 b Add one new word to each group.

2 Write what each of these pictures shows. Then use each word correctly in a sentence or short paragraph.

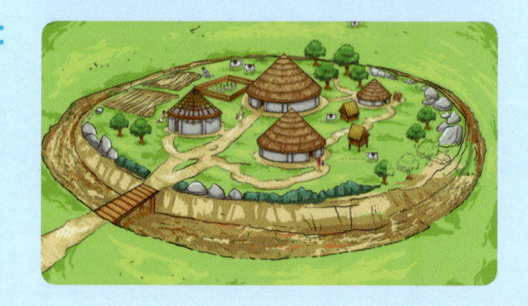

 a

 b

 c

60

3 Early civilisations

1 Match the words with the definitions.
   a a large group of people who live in an organised way
   b a city and the area of land around it
   c a line of rulers who come from the same family
   d the group of people with authority to organise and control a country or state

   > city-state   dynasty
   > government   society

2 Write a definition for each of the following words. Then use each word correctly in a sentence or short paragraph.
   a craftsperson
   b scribe
   c fertile
   d thatch
   e tablet

4 A history of communication

1 Complete each definition by choosing the correct ending from the box.
   a **papyrus** a writing material…
   b **moveable type** a printing method where characters are on separate blocks…
   c **newspaper** a daily or weekly publication of news and letters…
   d **communication** the act of delivering a message, news or information…
   e **invention** a new process or object…

   > …made from beaten fibres from a plant
   > …printed on folded sheets of paper
   > …that can be rearranged
   > …that did not previously exist
   > …using words, pictures or writing

2 Write what each of these pictures shows. Then use each word correctly in a sentence or short paragraph.

a
b
c
d
e
f

Vocabulary quiz

61

Glossary

archeologist a person who studies past human life, by looking at objects and other evidence

axe a tool with a blade for cutting down trees or chopping wood

bitumen a very thick, black, sticky liquid

broadcast a radio or television programme

Bronze Age the period of time after people discovered bronze, which they used to make tools, weapons and other objects

century one hundred years

charcoal a black material used for drawing and as fuel for fires

chariot a two-wheeled vehicle pulled by horses

city-state a city and the area of land around it

civilisation a place where people live and work together in a large, organised group

clan a close-knit group of related families

class a set of people within a society based on their wealth or position

communication the act of delivering a message, news or information through speech, drawing or writing

dam a barrier built across a river to hold back water

domesticate to teach to live and work with human beings

driftwood pieces of wood floating on the sea or carried by waves onto the shore

dyed treated so that the colour is changed

dynasty a line of rulers who come from the same family

event something important that happens

fertile land that can produce a large amount of crops

goods things that are useful to people such as food, tools and clothing

government the group of people with authority to organise and control a country or state

graphite a soft mineral used in pencils

hill fort an area of high ground with walls and ditches built around it, where people lived all the time or went for shelter during an attack

hunter-gatherers people who get their food by hunting animals and gathering plants

Ice Age a long period of low temperatures when thick ice covered much of the Earth

incense a dried paste of plant materials and oils that gives off a sweet smell when burned

invention a new process or object that did not previously exist

Iron Age the period when iron was used to make many different things that people needed

irrigation a man-made system for supplying water to crops

labourer a person who carries out unskilled manual work

linen a cloth woven from the flax plant

material what something is made of

mould a hollow container used to create objects by making the objects take a particular shape

moveable type a printing method where characters are on separate blocks that can be rearranged

natural resource something found in nature that people can use

newspaper a daily or weekly publication of news, articles and letters printed on folded sheets of paper

nomads people who move from one place to another instead of settling in one place

online available when connected to a network of computers

ore a mineral or rock containing metal

papyrus a writing material made from beaten fibres of the papyrus plant

peat squashed layers of very old, partly rotted plants found in damp ground

permanent lasting for a long time

plough a large farming tool used to cut through soil

port a town with a harbour and equipment for loading and unloading ships

postal service a service that delivers letters and parcels

pottery objects made from clay and baked to become hard

prehistoric a time in the past before people could write

printing the process of creating books or newspapers using moveable letter plates

radio a special way of sending signals that carry sound through the air

radio station a place with equipment for transmitting and receiving radio signals

reed a tall, thin grass that grows in wet ground

resource something that people can use

roundhouse a house built in a round shape because this shape was very strong

satellite an object placed in orbit around the Earth to transmit radio, television and telephone signals

scientist a person who studies the natural world by making observations and doing experiments

scribe a person who writes or copies out documents

scythe a tool with a long curved blade on a long handle used for cutting crops or grass

settlement a place where people live and make a community

shelter a place that gives protection from bad weather or danger

silk a fine, smooth fabric made from thread produced by silkworms

smart phone a mobile telephone that has many functions, like a computer

society a large group of people who live in an organised way

stable a building in which animals are kept

Stone Age a prehistoric period of time, when people made tools, weapons and other objects from stone

stylus an ancient writing tool, often with a sharp end for making marks and a blunt end for removing them

symbol a written character that represents a word or sound

tablet a flat piece of clay used to write on in ancient times

tax money collected to pay government workers, the army and for public services such as roads and water supply

technology using science to invent new things or to solve problems

terraced cut to form large 'steps' in a hillside

textiles woven or knitted cloth

thatch a roof covering of straw or reeds

timeline a way of showing events in order of when they happened, along a line

trade exchange one thing for something else

tribe a group of families and relatives who have the same language, customs and beliefs

turf a layer of grass and soil held together by grass and plant roots

word processor a machine for organising text entered using a keyboard, before the text is printed